QUALITY
SERVICE
TEAMWORK
and the quest for
EXCELLENCE

*the keys to
business success
in the 90's.*

QUALITY
SERVICE
TEAMWORK
and the quest for
EXCELLENCE

the keys to
business success
in the 90's.

CELEBRATING EXCELLENCE PUBLISHING

QUALITY, SERVICE, TEAMWORK
and the quest for EXCELLENCE

Book design by Michael McKee

ISBN: 1-880461-25-0

  5 6 7 8 Printing/AK/Year 97 96 95 94 93

TABLE OF CONTENTS

Quality

"Quality management is essential for survival in today's competitive business arena. The ability to create quality consciousness in a company is the foundation on which quality improvement must be built. Quality thought always precedes quality products and services."

Service

"To my customer: I may not have the answer, but I'll find it. I may not have the time, but I'll make it. I may not be the biggest, but I'll be the most committed to your success."

Teamwork

"Teamwork is the ability to work together toward a common vision. The ability to direct individual accomplishment toward organizational objectives. It is the fuel that allows common people to attain uncommon results. Simply stated, it is less me and more we."

Excellence

"Going far beyond the call of duty, doing more than others expect . . . this is what excellence is all about. And it comes from striving, maintaining the highest standards, looking after the smallest detail, and going the extra mile. Excellence means doing your very best. In everything. In every way."

*Dedicated to the customer . . .
the most important asset
of any business.*

PREFACE

"In today's world, companies will compete internationally only by improving internally. The battle cries of the 90's encourage commitment and cooperation, rallying the troops around a common cause. Individuals and organizations must meet the challenge to provide better products, exceed customer expectations and unite efforts. Quality, Service and Teamwork are not just slogans but the strategies to survive by. It is up to each of us to turn these purposeful words into professional reality."

QUALITY

"Quality management is essential for survival in today's competitive business arena. The ability to create quality consciousness in a company is the foundation on which quality improvement must be built. Quality thought always precedes quality products and services."

QUALITY SERVICE TEAMWORK
and the quest for
EXCELLENCE

"Quality is never an accident; it is always the result of high intention, sincere effort, intelligent direction and skillful execution; it represents the wise choice of many alternatives."

- WILL A. FOSTER

"If it ain't broke, fix it. Take fast. Make it faster. Take smart. Make it brilliant. Take good. Make it great."

- CIGNA ADVERTISEMENT

"Fix your eyes on perfection and you make almost everything speed towards it."

- W. E. CHANNING

"Quality is the first thing seen, service is the first thing felt and price is the first thing forgotten."

- JAY GOLTZ

"The customer is our final inspector."

"Imitators copy an idea; innovators build on it."

- DAN ZADRA

"We shall strive for excellence in all endeavors. We shall set our goals to achieve total customer satisfaction and to deliver defect-free premium value products on time, with service second to none."

"I spoke with an elderly Japanese assembly worker who found our concept of 'plus-or-minus' bewildering. He humbly explained that his sole tolerance was 'perfection.'"

- CAROLE O'REILLY

QUALITY
SERVICE
TEAMWORK
and the quest for
EXCELLENCE

"Thank God for competition. When our competitors upset our plans or outdo our designs, they open the infinite possibilities of our own work to us."

\- GIL ATKINSON

"Computers cannot tell you about the quality of your product . . . the human eye and human experience is the one thing that can make quality better . . . or poorer."

\- STANLEY MARCUS

"The measurement of quality is the price of non-conformance. 'Do it right the first time.'"

"The goal of quality is zero defects."

*"If you use your skill and imagination to see
how much you can give for a dollar,
instead of how little you can give for a dollar,
you are bound to succeed."*

- HENRY FORD

"Good enough is not 'good enough.'"

*"Few people go to work intending to perform poorly.
Managers must show them how to
pursue excellence."*

*"A company's commitment to quality makes people
proud to work there."*

QUALITY
SERVICE
TEAMWORK
and the quest for
EXCELLENCE

"*There is always a better way . . . your challenge is to find it.*"

"*Quality standards are contagious . . . spread them throughout the organization.*"

"*Nothing attracts customers like quality.*"

"*Quality marks the search for an ideal after necessity has been satisfied and mere usefulness achieved.*"

- WILL A. FOSTER

*"In his later years
Pablo Picasso was
not allowed to roam
an art gallery
unattended, for he had
previously been discovered
in the act of trying to
improve on one of his old
masterpieces."*

QUALITY
SERVICE
TEAMWORK
and the quest for
EXCELLENCE

"*It's amazing how close to perfection you can get if . . . you're willing to try.*"

"*When quality doesn't improve it usually means you're not dedicated enough.*"

"*Quality goes up when management has high expectations for their staff.*"

"*Excellence implies more than competence . . . it implies a striving for the highest possible standards.*"

"If quality is sacrificed, society is not truly served."

"Commitment to quality can be a great rallying force."

"There is a huge difference between 'the best money can buy' and 'the best value for the dollar.' Knowing which is most important to the customer is crucial."

"99% right is 100% wrong."

QUALITY
SERVICE
TEAMWORK
and the quest for
EXCELLENCE

"There is only one way to have a successful company . . . have a lot of happy, satisfied customers."

*"If **you** don't keep 'doing it better . . . ' your competition will."*

"When you're out of quality you're out of business."

"The system for creating quality is preventing, not appraising."

QUALITY
SERVICE
TEAMWORK
and the quest for
EXCELLENCE

"Quality only happens when you care enough to do your best."

"Pay attention to details. Sweat the small stuff."

"If things were done right only 99.9% of the time, we'd have two unsafe plane landings per day at O'Hare and 16,000 lost pieces of mail every hour by the U.S. Postal Service. Strive for 100% quality!"

- JEFF DEWAR

"Today's quality is tomorrow's future."

QUALITY
SERVICE
TEAMWORK
and the quest for
EXCELLENCE

"*Almost means not quite. Not quite means not right. Not right means wrong. Wrong means the opportunity to start again and get it right.*"

"Quality is a dynamic rather than a static process."

"The difference in failure and success is doing a thing nearly right and doing a thing exactly right."

"Our quality **'PERFORMANCE'** has not kept pace with our quality **'KNOWLEDGE.'**"

"Quality is never having to say you're sorry."

QUALITY
SERVICE
TEAMWORK
and the quest for
EXCELLENCE

"If better is possible, good is not enough."

"It is just the little difference between the good and the best that makes the difference between the artist and the artisan. It is just the little touches after the average man would quit that make the master's fame."

\- ORISON SWETT MARDEN

"Every job is a self-portrait of the person who did it. Autograph your work with quality."

"Quality is essentially attention to detail."

QUALITY
SERVICE
TEAMWORK
and the quest for
EXCELLENCE

"*There is only one rule of business and that is:
Make the best quality at the lowest cost possible.*"

\- HENRY FORD

"*It is quality rather than quantity
that matters.*"

\- SENECA

"*Quality is our most important product.*"

"*Don't try to sell what you have . . . rather have
what people need and value.*"

QUALITY
SERVICE
TEAMWORK
and the quest for
EXCELLENCE

"Quality products and services will never exceed that quality of the management team."

"Quality must not only exist . . . it must be perceived by the customer."

"Quality work reduces quality rework."

"Quality requires tenacity of purpose."

*"Just make up your
mind at the very outset that
your work is going to
stand for quality . . . that
you are going to stamp
a superior quality upon
everything that goes out
of your hands, that
whatever you do shall
bear the hallmark
of excellence."*

- ORISON SWETT MARDEN

QUALITY
SERVICE
TEAMWORK
and the quest for
EXCELLENCE

"*To produce quality you must have a 'system' to improve it.*"

"*It takes courageous leadership to admit that we must improve our quality.*"

"*Focus on quality.*"

"*Americans still care about quality. The country is full of intelligent, courageous people who would change if they only knew how.*"

- W. EDWARDS DEMING

"*Everyone must be <u>expected</u> to contribute ideas to improve quality.*"

"*Set quality improvement goals.*"

"*Your work is you. Don't let you down.*"

"*Quality levels must not only be attained but maintained, and improved.*"

QUALITY
SERVICE
TEAMWORK
and the quest for
EXCELLENCE

"A commitment to quality must start at the top."

"Most quality problems exist because we don't take the issue seriously enough."

"You must know the cost of poor quality."

"Quality products and services evolve from work environments."

- SAM L. MOORE

"Get rid of anyone who thinks quality standards 'are a pain in the neck.'"

"Every employee must know their contribution to quality."

"Much good work is lost for the lack of a little more."

- E. H. HARRIMAN

"Quality improvement is built on getting everyone to 'do it right the first time.'"

QUALITY
SERVICE
TEAMWORK
and the quest for
EXCELLENCE

"As you move forward, check each step for error. If you don't catch it, you inherit it."

"Constants aren't."

- JOHN PEERS

"Everything should be as simple as possible, but not simpler."

- ALBERT EINSTEIN

"When it comes to your product or project, people will take quality as seriously as you do — no more so."

- PHILIP B. CROSBY

"*Trifles make perfection, and perfection is no trifle.*"

\- MICHELANGELO

"*Good things happen when planned; bad things happen on their own.*"

\- *QUALITY IS FREE*

"*To lead a symphony, you must occasionally turn your back on the crowd.*"

"*Be quick but do not hurry.*"

\- JOHN WOODEN

QUALITY
SERVICE
TEAMWORK
and the quest for
EXCELLENCE

*"*R*eal quality is free."*

\- PHILIP CROSBY

*"*I*f you haven't got the time to do it right, when will you find the time to do it over?"*

*"*Q*uality is meeting our customers' requirements at all times and striving to exceed them whenever possible."*

*"*I*f you don't believe in quality . . . you'll never produce it."*

"*Quality is a hands-on proposition.*"

"*Anything that reduces quality can be prevented.*"

"*The guarantee of continuity is quality.*"
- CAPTAIN EDWARD RICKENBACKER

"*Quality is defined as a conformance to requirements.*"

QUALITY
SERVICE
TEAMWORK
and the quest for
EXCELLENCE

"*Quality is improved not only by those achieving excellence . . . but also by those who are trying.*"

"*Quality plus innovation equals success.*"

"*Quality assurance must be supported by quality improvement.*"

"*Quality must be active rather than reactive.*"

"I hope the day will never come when the American nation will be the champion of the status-quo."

- JOHN FOSTER DULLES

"Quality criteria must exist for every function."

"There can be no quality . . . without properly educated employees."

"Quality improvement is a never-ending process."

SERVICE

"To my customer: I may not have the answer, but I'll find it. I may not have the time, but I'll make it. I may not be the biggest, but I'll be the most committed to your success."

QUALITY
SERVICE
TEAMWORK
and the quest for
EXCELLENCE

"Here is a simple but powerful rule . . . always give people more than they expect to get."

\- NELSON BOSWELL

"It takes months to find a customer; seconds to lose one."

"Moments of truth tell the tale of success or failure. Every contact with the customer creates a lasting impression — for better or worse. Handle each opportunity with care."

"Customer service is the difference between the 'good' and the 'great' company."

"*Efficiency is doing a thing right. Effectiveness is doing the right thing. Great customer service requires both.*"

"*Better three hours too soon, than one minute too late.*"

\- SHAKESPEARE

"*Hold yourself responsible for higher standards than anybody else expects of you. Never excuse yourself.*"

\- HENRY WARD BEECHER

"*Listening: you can convey no greater honor than actually hearing what someone has to say.*"

\- PHILIP CROSBY

QUALITY
SERVICE
TEAMWORK
and the quest for
EXCELLENCE

"A sale is not something you pursue; it's what happens to you while you are immersed in serving your customer."

"Consumers are statistics. Customers are people."

\- STANLEY MARCUS

"Give the world the best that you have, and the best will come back to you."

\- MADELINE BRIDGES

"People may doubt what you say, but they always believe what you do."

"Always think of your customers as 'suppliers' first. Work closely with them so they can 'supply you' with the information you need to 'supply them' with the right products and services."

\- SUSIE MARTHALLER

*"If someone says **can't**, that shows you what to do."*

\- JOHN CAGE

"To give real service you must add something which cannot be bought or measured with money, and that is sincerity and integrity."

\- DONALD A. ADAMS

"We have forty million reasons . . . but not a single excuse."

\- RUDYARD KIPLING

QUALITY
SERVICE
TEAMWORK
and the quest for
EXCELLENCE

"*And then some . . .
These three little words are the
secret to success. They are the difference between
average people and top people in most companies.
The top people always do what is expected . . .
and then some . . .
They are thoughtful of others; they are considerate
and kind . . . and then some. They meet their
obligations and responsibilities
fairly and squarely . . .
and then some . . .
they are good friends and neighbors . . .
and then some. They can be counted
on in an emergency . . .
and then some . . .
I am thankful for people like this, for they
make the world more livable. Their spirit
of service is summed up in these little words . . .
and then some.*"

- CARL HOLMES

"Customer complaints are the schoolbooks from which we learn."

"You have to have your heart in the business, and the business in your heart."

- THOMAS J. WATSON, SR.

"Customer service means solid guarantees and maintenance programs."

"Goodwill is the one and only asset the competition cannot undersell or destroy."

- MARSHALL FIELD

QUALITY
SERVICE
TEAMWORK
and the quest for
EXCELLENCE

"Customer service means getting to the cause of customer problems rather than symptoms."

"Focus on one thing . . . the customer."

"We make a living by what we get, but we make a life by what we give."

"Customer service is training people how to serve clients in an outstanding fashion."

"Customer service means projecting a positive image."

"Rule #1: use your good judgment in all situations. There will be no additional rules."

- NORDSTROM (DEPARTMENT STORE)
  EMPLOYEE MANUAL

"Customer service means hiring people-sensitive employees."

"Always exceed the customer's expectations."

QUALITY
SERVICE
TEAMWORK
and the quest for
EXCELLENCE

"The best way to evaluate customer service? Ask them."

"Customer service is 'application' of our knowledge and philosophy. Slogans without action won't work."

"A customer that 'complains' is doing you a great service."

"Customer service is awareness of needs, problems, fears, and aspirations."

"A customer is the most important visitor on our premises. He is not dependent on us — we are dependent on him. He is not an outsider in our business — he is a part of it. We are not doing him a favor by serving him . . . he is doing us a favor by giving us the opportunity to do so."

"Customer service is a pleasant voice."

"Be sure people can be proud of your product or service."

"Service is the essence of greatness. All great men and women became great because they gave some talent or ability in the service of others. And no matter how small our talent, we too can contribute in some way to others — we too can become great."

"Customer service is measured!"

"*Customer service is a professional appearance.*"

"*Customer service is a commitment.*"

"*Customer service makes every client feel like 'the most important.'*"

"*The customer's evaluation of service is more important than your own.*"

QUALITY SERVICE TEAMWORK
and the quest for EXCELLENCE

*"*Customer service must be consistent."*

*"*Tell customers you appreciate their business."*

*"*Customer service means an organized
integrated effort."*

*"*The customer who doesn't complain but doesn't come back
is the one who hurts us."*

"Customer service requires rewarding your best customer 'servants.'"

"Everyone in the organization must serve the customer . . . or support someone who does."

"Customer service means that every employee knows that no one is more important than the customer."

"Never let a customer problem go unresolved."

*"For he that expects nothing shall not be disappointed,
but he that expects much — if he lives
and uses that in hand day by day —
shall be full to running over."*

- EDGAR CAYCE

"Empathize with customer's problems."

"Always think in terms of what the other person wants."

- JAMES VAN FLEET

*"If your imagination leads you to understand how
quickly people grant your requests when those requests
appeal to their self-interest, you can have
practically anything you go after."*

- NAPOLEON HILL

*"Treat each customer as an 'individual',
not a client."*

*"Eliminate customer 'surprises'. . .
unless they're pleasant ones!"*

"Customer service means quick response."

*"The only certain means of success is to render more and
better services than is expected of you, no matter what
your talk may be."*

\- OG MANDINO

QUALITY
SERVICE
TEAMWORK
and the quest for
EXCELLENCE

"R*ule #1
If we don't
take care of our customers . . .
somebody else will.*"

"Continually look for ways to improve quality and add value to products our customers purchase."

"No business can make a profit manufacturing something unless the customer can profit by using it."

\- SAM PETTENGILL

"Nothing is ever gained by winning an argument and losing a customer."

\- C. F. NORTON

"Your customers don't care how much you know . . . until they know how much you care."

\- GERHARD GSCHWANDTNER

QUALITY
SERVICE
TEAMWORK
and the quest for
EXCELLENCE

"Customer service is patience."

"Never be the reason a customer doesn't come back."

"If you paint in your mind a picture of bright and happy expectations, you put yourself into a condition conductive to your goal."

- NORMAN VINCENT PEALE

"The satisfied customer is our best business strategy."

*"*M*ake it easy for people to buy from you."*

*"*S*atisfied customers have purchased 'good feelings' or 'solutions to problems.'"*

*"*K*now your customer's buying motives."*

*"*P*erceived quality is based on what the customer expected."*

"Correct customer service problems immediately."

"Think and feel yourself there! To achieve any aim in life, you need to project the end-result . . . Think of the elation, the satisfaction, the joy! Carrying the ecstatic feeling will bring the desired goal into view."

\- GRACE SPEARE

"Customer service is a combination of little things."

"You never get a second chance to make a good first impression."

*"*Nobody ever won an argument
with a customer.*"*

*"*Hold discussion groups on service.*"*

*"*Customer service must be breathing in
every employee.*"*

*"*Look at your business through your customer's eyes.*"*

QUALITY
SERVICE
TEAMWORK
and the quest for
EXCELLENCE

"One of the most important principles of success is developing the habit of going the extra mile."

- NAPOLEON HILL

"Reputation is built by a thousand individual acts, and lost by merely one."

"The goal of customer service is to make people want to do business with us."

"The quality of any product or service is what the customer says it is."

*"*C*ustomer service is an attitude . . . the customer is our purpose for being."*

*"*A*sk how you might help your customers in the future."*

*"*M*ake it a 'joy' for people to do business with you."*

*"*A*sk everyone for service improvement ideas."*

QUALITY
SERVICE
TEAMWORK
and the quest for
EXCELLENCE

"The customer is our reason for being here."

*"Always be courteous and polite during
each customer contact."*

*"Always do more than is expected when you handle
a customer's problem."*

"Never promise more than we can deliver."

"Superior service is a day to day, person by person challenge. Today is the day . . . the challenge is yours."

"Make 'heros' out of people who deliver the best customer service."

"Customer service must be married to innovation because the customers needs and expectations will change."

"Nothing that is weak continues to serve."

- DAVID SEABURY

TEAMWORK

"Teamwork is the ability to work together toward a common vision. The ability to direct individual accomplishment toward organizational objectives. It is the fuel that allows common people to attain uncommon results. Simply stated, it is less me and more we."

QUALITY
SERVICE
TEAMWORK
and the quest for
EXCELLENCE

"*Many hands, hearts and minds generally contribute to anyone's notable achievements.*"

- WALT DISNEY

"*The secret is to work less as individuals and more as a team. As a coach, I play not my eleven best, but my best eleven.*"

- KNUTE ROCKNE

"*A hurricane: many individual raindrops cooperating.*"

"*Never doubt that a small group of thoughtful, committed people can change the world; indeed it is the only thing that ever has.*"

- MARGARET MEAD

*"We treat our people like royalty. If you
honor and serve the people who work for you,
they will honor and serve you."*

- MARY KAY ASH

"Who has not served cannot command."

- JOHN FLORIO

*"The great leader is not the one in the spotlight,
he's the one leading the applause."*

*"For decades great athletic teams have harbored one simple
secret that only a few select business teams have
discovered, and it is this: to play and win together,
you must practice together."*

- LEWIS EDWARDS

"Group desire is different than individual desire. With individual desire, it's up to you to feed the fire. With group desire, you get all kinds of people rolling logs on from every direction."

- VINCE PFAFF

"*No one can be the best at everything. But when all of us combine our talents, we can be the best at virtually anything.*"
- DON WARD

"*Innovation is simply group intelligence having fun.*"
- MICHAEL NOLAN

"*Diversity: the art of thinking independently together.*"
- MALCOLM FORBES

"*As an organization grows it must be more human, not less.*"
- SWIFT & CO., CIRCA 1920

QUALITY
SERVICE
TEAMWORK
and the quest for
EXCELLENCE

"Coming together is a beginning, staying together is progress, and working together is success."

"Great discoveries and achievements invariably involve the cooperation of many minds."

- ALEXANDER GRAHAM BELL

"If you're too busy to help those around you succeed, you're too busy."

"Working together works."

*"You don't always have to like each other, but
you have to be able to count on each other. When
my team calls on me, I'll be ready. When they set
the ball down, I'll put it through."*

- GEORGE BLANDA
  NFL KICKER

*"There is no limit to what you can do if you
don't care who gets the credit."*

*"Either we're pulling together or we're
pulling apart."*

*"The greatest good we can do for others is not to share
our riches but to reveal theirs."*

QUALITY
SERVICE
TEAMWORK
and the quest for
EXCELLENCE

"Together we can change the world."

"He who reflects on other men's insights will come easily by what they labored hard for."

"My green thumb came only as a result of the mistakes I made while learning to see things from the plant's point of view."

\- H. FRED ALE

"You become successful by helping others become successful."

*"*T*he Master*
Mind Principle:
two or more people actively
engaged in pursuit of a definite
purpose with a positive mental
attitude, constitute an
unbeatable force."

\- NAPOLEON HILL

QUALITY
SERVICE
TEAMWORK
and the quest for
EXCELLENCE

"No general can fight his battles alone. He must depend upon his lieutenants, and his success depends upon his ability to select the right man for the right place."

– L. OGDEN ARMOUR

"One man's word is no man's word; we should quietly hear all sides."

"Come now, and let us reason together."

– THE BIBLE

"To accept good advice from others is but to increase one's own ability."

"A person too busy to take care of his co-workers is like a mechanic too busy to take care of his tools."

"A team player tries to learn from those who are superior to him."

"Anything one man can imagine, other men can make real."

- JULES VERNE

"Doing nothing for others is the undoing of ourselves."

- HORACE MANN

QUALITY
SERVICE
TEAMWORK
and the quest for
EXCELLENCE

"A company is known by the people it keeps."

"Every great person is always being helped by everybody; for their gift is to get good out of all things and all persons."

— RUSKIN

"Winners can tell you where they are going, what they plan to do along the way and who will be sharing the adventure with them."

— DENIS WAITLEY

"In heroic organizations, people mentor each other unselfishly."

"*World's greatest management principle: you can work miracles by having faith in others. To get the best out of people, choose to think and believe the best about them.*"

"*As a rule of thumb, involve everyone in everything.*"

\- TOM PETERS

"*Americans will reach the moon by standing on each other's shoulders.*"

"T E. A. M. = *Together Everyone Achieves More.*"

\- JIM SULLIVAN
CELEBRATING EXCELLENCE
CREDIT MANAGER

QUALITY
SERVICE
TEAMWORK
and the quest for
EXCELLENCE

"Give all the credit away."

- JOHN WOODEN

"Be a go-giver as well as a go-getter."

- WHITT SCHULTZ

"I've learned one important thing about living. I can do anything I think I can — but I can't do anything alone. No one can go it alone. Create your team!"

- DR. ROBERT SCHULLER

"No matter what accomplishments you make somebody helps you."

- WILMA RUDOLPH

"The best thing to hold on to in life is each other."

"Asking for help is a strength, not a weakness."

*"Everyone has an invisible sign hanging from their neck that reads **Make Me Feel Important!** Never forget this message when working with people."*

"A job worth doing is worth doing together."

QUALITY
SERVICE
TEAMWORK
and the quest for
EXCELLENCE

"*Working together,
ordinary people can
perform extraordinary feats.
They can push things that
come into their hands a little
higher up, a little further on
towards the heights
of excellence.*"

"A successful team beats with one heart."

"Teamwork divides the task and doubles the success."

"No one can whistle a symphony. It takes an orchestra to play it."

- H. E. LUCCOCK

"We didn't all come over in the same ship, but we're all in the same boat."

- BERNARD M. BARUCH

QUALITY
SERVICE
TEAMWORK
and the quest for
EXCELLENCE

"The team player knows that it doesn't matter who gets the credit as long as the job gets done. If the job gets done, the credit will come."

- THE EDGE

"The best minute you spend is the one you invest in people."

- BLANCHARD AND JOHNSON

"There is no exercise better for the heart than reaching down and lifting people up."

- JOHN A. HOLMES

"Shared value is the unifying force of a team."

"Individuals say 'I'. . .teams say 'we.'"

"Big ideas are so hard to recognize, so fragile, so easy to kill. Don't forget that, all of you who don't have them."

\- JOHN ELLIOT, JR.
  OGILVY & MATHER ADVERTISING

"A company is like a ship. Everyone ought to be prepared to take the helm."

\- MORRIS WEEKS

"None of us is as smart as all of us."

\- KEN BLANCHARD

QUALITY
SERVICE
TEAMWORK
and the quest for
EXCELLENCE

"It takes two wings for a bird to fly."

- JESSE JACKSON

"The world basically and fundamentally is constituted on the basis of harmony. Everything works in cooperation with something else."

- PRESTON BRADLEY

"Team success and individual success can be synonymous."

"A team without goals is just another ineffective committee."

"Team leadership impacts team performance."

"Humor is a great lubricant for teamwork."

"I know of no great man except those who have rendered great services to the human race."

"Here is a basic rule for winning success. Let's mark it in the mind and remember it. The rule is: success depends on the support of other people. The only hurdle between you and what you want to be is the support of others."
- DAVID JOSEPH SCHWARTZ

QUALITY
SERVICE
TEAMWORK
and the quest for
EXCELLENCE

"A *team leader must set an example*
for others to follow."

"The *coach is the team, and the team is the*
coach. You reflect each other."

- SPARKY ANDERSON

"The *achievements of an organization are the result of*
the combined effort of each individual."

- VINCENT T. LOMBARDI

"A *team will out perform a group of*
individuals every time."

"Never let an individual dominate a team."

"Teams should compete with themselves to do more and to do better."

"Our future will be a reflection of our teamwork."

"Innovation creates opportunity, quality creates demand, but it takes teamwork to make it happen."

QUALITY
SERVICE
TEAMWORK
and the quest for
EXCELLENCE

"If I have been able to see farther than others, it is because I have stood on the shoulders of giants."

- SIR ISAAC NEWTON

"The object is not to see through one another, but to see one another through."

- PETER DEVRIES

"It is one of the beautiful compensations of this life that no one can sincerely try to help another without helping himself."

- CHARLES DUDLEY WARNER

"Those convinced against their will are of the same opinion still."

- DALE CARNEGIE

"The best leaders are very often the best listeners. They have an open mind. They are not interested in having their own way but in finding the best way."

- WILFRED PETERSON

"He has the right to criticize who has the heart to help."

- ABRAHAM LINCOLN

"Everyone appreciates being appreciated. Try to catch people red-handed in the act of doing something right — and praise them for it."

- BOB MOAWAD

"There is no higher religion than human service. To work for the common good is the greatest creed."

- ALBERT SCHWEITZER

QUALITY
SERVICE
TEAMWORK
and the quest for
EXCELLENCE

"We are in this life together."

"The best team doesn't win nearly as often as the team that gets along best."

\- DR. ROB GILBERT

"The main ingredient of stardom is the rest of the team."

\- JOHN WOODEN

"If everyone is moving forward together, then the success takes care of itself."

\- HENRY FORD

"A great manager has a knack for making players think they're better than they think they are. Once you learn how good you really are, you never settle for playing less than your best."

- REGGIE JACKSON

"Praise loudly and blame softly."

"What affects everyone can best be solved by everyone."

"People support what they help create."

QUALITY
SERVICE
TEAMWORK
and the quest for
EXCELLENCE

"When love and skill work together,
expect a masterpiece."

— C. READE

"Celebrate what you want to see more of."

— TOM PETERS

"A team of giants needs giant pitchers who throw good
ideas. But every great pitcher needs an outstanding
catcher. Without giant catchers, the ideas of giant
pitchers may eventually disappear."

— MAX DE PREE
LEADERSHIP IS AN ART

"Companies don't succeed . . . people do."

*"There are precious few Einsteins among us.
Most brilliance arises from ordinary people
working together in extraordinary ways."*

- ROGER VON OECH

"Working together means winning together."

*"Teamwork is the fuel that allows common people
to attain uncommon results."*

"Teamwork . . . More 'we' and less 'me'."

EXCELLENCE

"Going far beyond the call of duty, doing more than others expect . . . this is what excellence is all about. And it comes from striving, maintaining the highest standards, looking after the smallest detail, and going the extra mile. Excellence means doing your very best. In everything. In every way."

87

QUALITY
SERVICE
TEAMWORK
and the quest for
EXCELLENCE

"The quality of a person's life is in direct proportion to their commitment to excellence, regardless of their chosen field of endeavor."

\- VINCENT T. LOMBARDI

"The difference between failure and success is doing a thing nearly right and doing a thing exactly right."

\- EDWARD SIMMONS

"Don't measure yourself by what you have accomplished, but by what you should have accomplished with your ability."

"Excellence can be attained if you . . . Care more than others think is wise. Risk more than others think is safe. Dream more than others think is practical. Expect more than others think is possible."

"*The human mind, once stretched by a new idea,
never regains its original dimensions.*"

- OLIVER WENDELL HOLMES

"*It's been said that all great discoveries are
made by those whose feelings run
ahead of their thinking.*"

"*Discovery is seeing what everybody else has seen,
and thinking what nobody else has thought.*"

- ALBERT SZENT-GYORGI

"*It's amazing what ordinary people can do if they set out
without preconceived notions.*"

- CHARLES F. KETTERING

QUALITY
SERVICE
TEAMWORK
and the quest for
EXCELLENCE

"*You are successful the moment you start moving toward a worthwhile goal.*"

- CHUCK CARLSON

"*Every thought is a seed. If you plant 'Crab' apples, don't count on harvesting 'Golden Delicious'.*"

- THE EDGE

"*Imagination is the highest kite you can fly.*"

- LAUREN BACALL

"*For every obstacle there is a solution — over, under, around or through.*"

" You can't build a reputation on what you're going to do."

- HENRY FORD

" Those who say it can't be done are usually interrupted by those who are doing it."

" If you can dream it, you can do it."

- WALT DISNEY

" Life is no brief candle to me. It is a sort of splendid torch which I have got hold of for the moment, and I want to make it burn as brightly as possible before handing it on to future generations."

- GEORGE BERNARD SHAW

QUALITY
SERVICE
TEAMWORK
and the quest for
EXCELLENCE

"*P*ride is a personal commitment. It is an attitude which separates excellence from mediocrity. It is that ingredient which inspires us not to get ahead of others, but rather to get ahead of ourselves."

"*T*he seeds of great discoveries are constantly floating around, but they only take root in minds well prepared to receive them."

- JOSEPH HENRY

"*D*esire is the key to motivation, but it's the determination and commitment to an unrelenting pursuit of your goal — a commitment to excellence — that will enable you to attain the success you seek."

- MARIO ANDRETTI

"*N*othing binds us one to the other like a promise kept. Nothing divides us like a promise broken."

- MASS MUTUAL

QUALITY
SERVICE
TEAMWORK
and the quest for
EXCELLENCE

"*D*o not wish to be anything but what you
are, and try to be that perfectly."

\- ST. FRANCIS DE SALES

"*S*ome men dream of worthy accomplishments,
while others stay awake and do them."

"*T*o dream anything that you want to dream; that
is the beauty of the human mind. To do anything that
you want to do; that is the strength of the human
will. To trust yourself to test your limits; that is
the courage to succeed."

\- BERNARD EDMONDS

"*A*ll glory comes from daring to begin."

\- EUGENE F. WARE

QUALITY
SERVICE
TEAMWORK
and the quest for
EXCELLENCE

"We are what we repeatedly do. Excellence, then, is not an act but a habit."

"Well done is better than well said."

- BEN FRANKLIN

"Unless you try to do something beyond what you have already mastered, you will never grow."

- RONALD E. OSBORN

"The ultimate victory in competition is derived from the inner satisfaction of knowing that you have done your best and that you have gotten the most out of what you had to give."

- HOWARD COSELL

QUALITY
SERVICE
TEAMWORK
and the quest for
EXCELLENCE

"*Many of life's failures are men who did not realize how close they were to success when they gave up.*"

"*I am a big believer in the 'mirror test.' All that matters is if you can look in the mirror and honestly tell the person you see there, that you've done your best.*"

- JOHN McCAY

"*Reach beyond your grasp. Your goals should be grand enough to get the best of you.*"

- TEILHARD DE CHARDIN

"*When we have done our best, we should wait the result in peace.*"

- JOHN LUBBOCK

QUALITY
SERVICE
TEAMWORK
and the quest for
EXCELLENCE

"Some people see things as they are and say 'Why?' I dream things that never were, and say 'Why not?'"

\- GEORGE BERNARD SHAW

"It's what you learn after you know it all that counts."

\- JOHN WOODEN

"A winner is someone who sets his goals, commits himself to those goals, and then pursues his goals with all the ability given him."

"We could all take a lesson from the great northern geese which fly thousands of miles in perfect formation. Formation flying is 70% more efficient than flying alone."

"*A total commitment is paramount to reaching the ultimate in performance.*"

- TOM FLORES

"*The price of success is hard work, dedication to the job at hand, and the determination that whether we win or lose, we have applied the best of ourselves to the task at hand.*"

- VINCENT T. LOMBARDI

"*The greatest thing in this world is not so much where we are, but in what direction we are moving.*"

- OLIVER WENDELL HOLMES

"*Keep a diary or daily win book to record your aspirations and accomplishments. If your life is worth living, it's worth recording.*"

QUALITY
SERVICE
TEAMWORK
and the quest for
EXCELLENCE

"The spirit, the will to win, and the will to excel are the things that endure. These qualities are so much more important than the events that occur."

— VINCENT T. LOMBARDI

"There are four steps to accomplishment: Plan purposefully. Prepare prayerfully. Proceed positively. Pursue persistently."

"Only those who dare to fail greatly can ever achieve greatly."

"One man has enthusiasm for 30 minutes, another for 30 days, but it is the man who has it for 30 years who makes a success of his life."

— EDWARD B. BUTLER

"The secret of success in life is for a man to be ready for his opportunity when it comes."

- BENJAMIN DISRAELI

"I do the best I know how, the very best I can; and I mean to keep on doing it to the end. If the end brings me out all right, what is said against me will not amount to any thing. If the end brings me out all wrong, ten angels swearing I was right would make no difference."

- ABRAHAM LINCOLN

"People forget how fast you did a job — but they remember how well you did it."

"One of life's most painful moments comes when we must admit that we didn't do our homework, that we are not prepared."

- MERLIN OLSON

QUALITY
SERVICE
TEAMWORK
and the quest for
EXCELLENCE

"Never, Never, Never Quit."

\- WINSTON CHURCHILL

"If you don't invest very much, then defeat doesn't hurt very much and winning is not very exciting."

\- DICK VERMEIL

"Our chief want in life is somebody who will make us do what we can."

\- RALPH WALDO EMERSON

"I always view problems as opportunities in work clothes."

\- HENRY KAISER

"If a man is called to be a streetsweeper, he should sweep streets as Michelangelo painted, or Beethoven composed music, or Shakespeare wrote poetry. He should sweep streets so well that all the hosts of heaven and earth will pause to say, here lived a great streetsweeper who did his job well."

- MARTIN LUTHER KING JR.

QUALITY
SERVICE
TEAMWORK
and the quest for
EXCELLENCE

"To succeed — do the best you can, where you are, with what you have."

"Men are often capable of greater things than they perform. They are sent into the world with bills of credit, and seldom draw to full extent."

\- WALPOLE

"Winning isn't everything — it's the only thing."

\- VINCENT T. LOMBARDI

"The difference between the impossible and the possible lies in a man's determination."

\- TOMMY LASORDA

"*A great pleasure in life is doing what people say you cannot do.*"

\- WALTER GAGEHOT

"*Ingenuity, plus courage, plus work, equals miracles.*"

\- BOB RICHARDS

"*The road to success is paved with good intentions.*"

"*If you've made up your mind you can do something, you're absolutely right.*"

QUALITY
SERVICE
TEAMWORK
and the quest for
EXCELLENCE

"Do not let what you cannot do interfere with what you can do."

- JOHN WOODEN

"Real leaders are ordinary people with extraordinary determination."

"Enthusiasm is the propelling force necessary for climbing the ladder of success."

"We cannot direct the wind . . . but we can adjust the sails."

QUALITY
SERVICE
TEAMWORK
and the quest for
EXCELLENCE

"Two men look through the self-same bars; one sees mud, and one sees the stars."

- FREDERICK LANGBRIDGE

"Failure is not the worst thing in the world. The very worst is not to try."

"The harder you work the luckier you get."

- GARY PLAYER

"The only time you can't afford to fail is the last time you try."

- CHARLES KETTERING

QUALITY
SERVICE
TEAMWORK
and the quest for
EXCELLENCE

"Take fast and make it faster. Take smart and make it brilliant. Believe that no matter how well you do something, you can always do it better. And chances are you will."

"*Act as though it were impossible to fail.*"

"*The man who goes farthest is generally the one who is willing to do and dare. The 'sure thing boat' never gets far from shore.*"

- DALE CARNEGIE

"*Purpose is the engine that fires your dream and your team.*"

"*It takes courage to push yourself to places that you have never been before . . . to test your limits . . . to break through barriers.*"

QUALITY
SERVICE
TEAMWORK
and the quest for
EXCELLENCE

"There is always room at the top."

— DANIEL WEBSTER

"Don't be afraid to take a big step if one is indicated. You can't cross a chasm in two small jumps."

— DAVID LLOYD GEORGE

"He is great who can do what he wishes; he is wise who wishes to do what he can."

"Nothing great will ever be achieved without great men, and men are great only if they are determined to be so."

— CHARLES DE GAULLE

"Accept the challenges, so that you may feel the exhilaration of victory."

- GENERAL GEORGE S. PATTON

"People seldom improve when they have no other model but themselves to copy after."

- GOLDSMITH

"The difference between ordinary and extraordinary is that little extra."

"Paralyze resistance with persistence."

- WOODY HAYES

QUALITY
SERVICE
TEAMWORK
and the quest for
EXCELLENCE

"The real friend of his country is the person who believes in excellence, seeks for it, fights for it, defends it and tries to produce it."

- MORLEY CALLAGHAN

"If you can't do great things, do small things in a great way. Don't wait for great opportunities. Seize common, everyday ones and make them great."

- NAPOLEON HILL

"Don't care what others think of what you do; but care very much about what you think you do."

"I have been given this day to use as I will. I can waste it or use it for good. What I choose to do is important, because I am exchanging a day of my life for it."

"*Use the word 'impossible' with great caution.*"

- WERNER VON BRAUN

"*Whatever a man can be, he ought to be.*"

- ABRAHAM MASLOW

"*No job on earth is insignificant if it is accomplished with pride and artistry. 'The french fry is my canvas,' said McDonald's founder Ray Kroc. 'What's your canvas?'*"

"*People don't give a hoot about who made the original whatzit. They want to know who makes the best one.*"

- HOWARD W. NEWTON

QUALITY
SERVICE
TEAMWORK
and the quest for
EXCELLENCE

"*To love what you do and feel that it matters — how could anything be more fun?*"

— KATHERINE GRAHAM

"*One person with a belief is equal to a force of ninety-nine who have only interests.*"

— JOHN STUART HILL

"*Formula for success: underpromise and overdeliver.*"

— TOM PETERS

"*The fight is won or lost far away from witnesses — behind the lines, in the gym and out there on the road, long before I dance under those lights.*"

— MOHAMMAD ALI

"*Don't compromise yourself.
You are all you've got.*"

- BETTY FORD

"*Some succeed because they are destined to;
most succeed because they are
determined to.*"

"*The real winners in life are the people who look at
every situation with an expectation that they
can make it work or make it better.*"

- BARBARA PLETCHER

"*Advice from a veteran trapeze performer:
'Throw your heart over the bars and your body will follow.'*"

QUALITY
SERVICE
TEAMWORK
and the quest for
EXCELLENCE

"You can out do you — if you really want to."

- PAUL HARVEY

"Sign seen in a University of Washington oceanography class: 'Man is 97% water; the rest is all attitude.'"

"Give what you have. To someone, it may be better than you dare think."

- LONGFELLOW

"Whenever the human adventure reaches great and complete expression, we can be sure it is because someone has dared to be his unaverage self."

- RAE NOEL

"No one ever attains
very eminent success
by simply doing what is
required of him; it is
the amount and excellence
of what is over and above
the required that
determines the greatness
of ultimate distinction."

- CHARLES KENDALL ADAMS

QUALITY
SERVICE
TEAMWORK
and the quest for
EXCELLENCE

"Hope sees the invisible, feels the intangible and achieves the impossible."

"Great minds must be ready not only to take opportunities, but to make them."

\- COLTON

"The man who cannot believe in himself cannot believe in anything else."

\- ROY L. SMITH

"Today's preparation determines tomorrow's achievement."

"*When an archer misses the mark, he turns and looks for the fault within himself. Failure to hit the bull's-eye is never the fault of the target. To improve your aim — improve yourself.*"

- GILBERT ARLAND

"*Good is not good where better is expected.*"

- THOMAS FULLER

"*Choice, not chance, determines destiny.*"

"*You will become as small as your controlling desire, as great as your dominant aspiration.*"

- JAMES ALLEN

QUALITY
SERVICE
TEAMWORK
and the quest for
EXCELLENCE

"Leadership is the courage to admit mistakes, the vision to welcome change, the enthusiasm to motivate others and the confidence to stay out of step when everyone else is marching to the wrong tune."

- E. M. ESTES

"For lack of training, they lacked knowledge. For lack of knowledge, they lacked confidence. For lack of confidence, they lacked victory."

- JULIUS CAESAR

"Failure is impossible."

- SUSAN B. ANTHONY

"I start where the last man left off."

- THOMAS A. EDISON

"*When it comes to your product or project,
people will take quality as seriously as
you do — no more so.*"

- PHILIP B. CROSBY

"*Though the talents you possess may appear
to be average or less, use them anyway. The woods
would be very silent if no birds sang except
the very best.*"

"*I could not sleep when I got on the hunt for an
idea, until I had caught it. This was a kind of passion
with me, and it has stuck with me.*"

- ABRAHAM LINCOLN

"*Do not follow where the path may lead. Go instead
where there is no path and leave a trail.*"

OTHER BOOKS FROM CELEBRATING EXCELLENCE

Commitment to Excellence

Management Magic

Business Quotes

Motivational Quotes

Customer Care

Opportunity Selling

The Best of Success

Great Quotes from Great Leaders

Commitment to Quality

America: It's People, It's Pride and It's Progress

Great Quotes from Great Women

Zig Ziglar's Favorite Quotations

Think: Creativity and Innovation

Winning With Teamwork

The Power of Goals

Your Attitude Determines Your Altitude

Never, Never Quit

CELEBRATING EXCELLENCE PUBLISHING